Milo Yiannopoulos at LeWeb'13 Conference at Methodist
Central Hall, Westminster in London on June 5, 2013.
Photo by Kmeron for LeWeb13 Conference.

MILO YIANNOPOULOS
& All This Mess

NeoPopRealismPRESS

Milo Yiannopoulos at LeWeb'13 Conference at Methodist
Central Hall, Westminster in London. June 2013.
Photo by Kmeron.

First published by NeoPopRealism PRESS in 2017
Copyright © Neopoprealism Press, 2017

Printed in the United States of America

ISBN-13: 9781544626604
ISBN-10: 1544626606

Language: English
Author: NeoPopRealism Press
MILO YIANNOPOULOS & All This Mess

Cover photo by Kmeron for LeWeb13 Conference. Milo Yiannopoulos appears at LeWeb'13 Conference at Methodist Central Hall, Westminster in London on June 5, 2013.

This book is a work of non-fiction. The contents of this book are true.

NeoPopRealism PRESS, PO BOX 366, New York NY, 10013

NeoPopRealism PRESS books are available at special discounts for bulk purchases. For more information contact through the publisher's website www.neopoprealism.org

17 16 15 14 13   10 9 8 7 6 5 4 3 2 1

CONTENT

MILO YIANNOPOULOS

& All This Mess

NeoPopRealismPress

9

1

Politics Could Be Entertaining

I haven't heard of Milo Yiannopoulos until February of 2017, but I found out a lot of things about him during this short period of time because it was the most dynamic period of his life, at least by now. My first impression of him when I saw Milo for the first time when he was interviewed on Fox TV by Tucker Carlson about the protests at

Berkeley against his speech was difficult to characterize. I was stunned. I was stunned by what was going on at Berkeley, by what Milo said and the way he said it. It was not a regular mainstream media interview. It was refreshing to watch someone like Milo after years of dull stuff coming throughout all TV channels on daily basis, no wonder he created such turmoil. I stopped watching TV long time ago because even the prospectively new things were always filtered, twisted and not fun to listen and watch. The bright colors of the common sense were brushed out. Stupidity and "carry on" agenda to do what a "big brother" tells you to do were promoted widely by all mainstream media outlets among all ages individuals, often suggesting even inappropriate things. Many, mostly of whose who were mentally weak, uneducated or not experienced enough, accepted this "carry on" agenda as inevitable, which is a dramatic thing for a free society.

Yiannopoulos was fabulous, but I cannot say that I accepted immediately everything about him. However, he was the air freshener in a stinky toilet, the life-saver for the suffocated. I did not know that he was a gay when I saw him for the first time, and some of his manners seemed to me not natural. But now, when I know that he is not a straight man, I understand where they came from.

The most fascinating thing about Milo is that he makes you think. It happens because he regularly says a lot and on different subjects, and you need to comprehend quickly what he said, connecting it to your life experiences or to what you do know about it from other sources. He makes you not only think about what he said, but also makes you active. He makes you start your own search for the truth and the common sense. He gives you the brain's training sessions showing that there is a bunch of things you need to think about before you would come to any conclusion. He, who is intelligent and humorous at the same time, turns his "training sessions" (speeches) into fun if not a pleasure. Everyone likes humor. And who could know that politics could be so entertaining! Because politics with Yiannopoulos are not boring, more people are willing to get into it, exploring different subjects, views, and even doctrines.

2

How Milo Got Himself Into Hot Water

Low did this happen that intelligent and entertaining Milo Yiannopoulos got himself into hot water and was targeted by both the left and conservatives at the same time? And why was his CPAC's speech cancelled? Is this a big deal? And is this a big deal that his upcoming book "Dangerous" has been canceled by the "Simon & Schuster"?

Several months ago, Milo was interviewed by the "Drunken Peasants," and during this interview he was talking about his first sexual experiences at age 13. His partners were "slightly" older, they were in their late 20s or so. Milo lost his virginity to a male, who was a drag queen. His second partner seemed was a priest, and Milo jokes about it a lot. Somehow he had the positive memories of his relationships with a priest because those relationships stimulated Milo's intellectuality. It seems that Milo did not see himself as a child when he was 13. Even now, he still thinks he was then like an adult because he matured sexually faster than other boys. Or may be he just does not want to think the other way because subconsciously he does not want to see himself as a victim of a child abuse. But the fact is, Milo verbally expressed his positive feelings toward priest's role in his intellectual growth, saying that there was a possibility that some "younger boys" could benefit from their relationships with the "older men". These words caused an explosion. His words' choice was not careful. Even if he wanted to provoke some reaction or debate, he could do better with a grotesque, choosing the right words.

15

This old interview was turned against Milo as the left could say "at the right time". This interview was pushed to everyone's attention right before CPAC (Conservative Political Action Conference), which took place February 24, 2017. It was made with a purpose to "expose" Yiannopoulos' "dark side" as a pedophilia supporter, even it was an absurd, as there was no evidence in the real world that he supports pedophilia. Opposite, he has exposed three pedophiles and advocated for sexual abuse survivors. However, many people were mislead by the mainstream media with fake news articles.

Yiannopoulos was disinvited from CPAC as a speaker right after his appearance on HBO Maher's Real Time show, which was aired a few days before CPAC. Milo's appearance at this show with a shining smile when talking to Maher could be a reason why he was disinvited from the Conservative Political Action Conference. It was a great addition to a video in which he was talking about his sexual partner priest positively. Some older conservatives could come to a conclusion: "Maher and Milo found each other, way to go guys.

Good bye, Milo, you belong to the left." The Conservatives probably would not want to be associated with anyone and anything related to pedophilia and Mr. Maher, who was a leftist, supporting pedophilia in his own show years ago, even without any bad consequences.

Many years ago, Maher was talking at his show favorably about a female-pedophile, a school teacher who was in jail because "she was in love". This is how Maher felt about the situation. She was in her 30s and her sexual partner - a school student, with whom she had a little child and was pregnant again - was 12-13 years old when they started. Then Maher was interpreted by many as the pedophilia supporter, and older conservatives remembered it. Additionally to everything, before and after the recent US's election, there has been a lot of talk about pedophiles spotted among top officials democrats, including in Washington DC, and also among Hollywood's celebrities, and many people started automatically associate the subject of pedophilia with leftists. A combination of two - the Yiannopoulos' appearance at the Maher's Real Time show and his comment on his relationship with priest Michael in "Drunken Peasants" Interview - could be a turning point leading to canceling his speech at CPAC.

But is this a big deal for the Libertarians and Conservatives what happened to Milo? It is difficult to overestimate Milo's investment in the current US's politics. It cannot be forgotten already because together with some others he shook the "sinking ship" (the US) and woke the sleeping sheep and couch potatoes up using the right to free speech. And the world would never be the same again because with help of such individuals as Milo, Ann Coulter, Ben Shapiro, Lauren Southern, and others, Donald J. Trump became the US's President. America woke up from inside, but the losers are still trying to put the blame on Russians.

What has happened to Yiannopoulos' career could be a big deal for him personally because he needs now some time to put things together. His book "Dangerous" should come out with another publisher because the "Simon & Schuster" is not the only publishing company in America. They made a silly statement by canceling one of the prospectively best of their books. Milo's book in its pre-order state and at the moment of its cancellation was a #1 bestselling book at Amazon.

3
History & Ages
of Consent

We all go sometimes through all kinds of crazy things and situations in life, including related to relationships and of course sex. Sex is a sphere in which each individual needs some personal discoveries, unless everything goes smooth itself or there is no interest to it at all. However, sex is not the most important part of our lives (should be), even some "scientists" and quite obsessive practitioners want to suggest the other things to the silently or not silently cracking their sexuality code majority (sexual relationships between different or same sexes and the consequences). The age of consent in many countries probably is too low, and this fact negatively reflects on the people's lives, unless they feel and think like the rabbits. The most life's confusions, problems, and miseries actually come from the relationships and particularly sexual relationships and interactions with all those rejections and sexual desire (sometimes constant among sexoholics). All people are so different, and it is not easy to find the right person-partner in this complex world, especially when polygamy is promoted widely, but we all still have the ego, even to a different extend. The majority of people experience all kinds of failures, even they do not want to admit them and live their lives with or married to the partners they do not love or care about. Think about all that for a while, try to analyze how your sexuality and your needs in sexual relationships have affected your life, positive or negative, or both. May be it is better to start later and quit earlier? I did. And it feels great. Sex after marriage actually is also a great idea, even many people think it is too old fashion.

The distinguishing aspect of the age of consent

laws is that the person below the minimum age is regarded as the victim, and their sex partner as the offender. And the age of consent today varies depending on country, it is mostly in the range from 14 to 18. It was not always that way. If we would go back in history, we would see how the age of consent was changing. In the 12th century, Gratian, the influential founder of canon law in medieval Europe, accepted age of puberty for marriage to be around 12 (girls) and around 14 (boys) but acknowledged consent to be meaningful if the children were older than 7. There were authorities that said that consent could take place earlier. Marriage would then be valid as long as neither of the two parties annulled the marital agreement before reaching puberty, or if they had already consummated the marriage. Judges sometimes honored marriages based on mutual consent at ages younger than 7: in contrast to established canon, there are recorded marriages of 2 and 3 year olds. The first recorded age-of-consent law dates from 1275 in England; as part of its provisions on rape, the Statute of *Westminster 1275* made it a misdemeanor to "ravish" a "maiden within age," whether with or without her consent. The phrase "within age" was later interpreted by jurist Sir Edward Coke as meaning the age of marriage, which at the time was 12 years of age. The American colonies followed the English tradition, and the law was more of a guide. For example, Mary Hathaway (Virginia, 1689) was only 9 when she was married to William Williams. Sir Edward Coke (England, 17th century) *made it clear that the marriage of girls under 12 was normal, and the age at which a girl, who was a wife was eligible for a dower from her husband's estate, was 9, even though her husband be only four years old.* " In the 16th century, a few Italian and German states set 12 years old as the minimum age for sexual intercourse for girls. Toward the end of the 18th century, other European countries also began to enact similar laws. The first French Constitution of 1791 established the minimum age at 11 years old. Portugal, Spain, Denmark and the Swiss cantons initially set the minimum age at 10–12 years old. Age of consent laws were difficult to follow and enforce: legal norms based on age were not, in general, common until the 19th century, because clear proof of exact age and precise date of birth were often unavailable.

In Christian societies, sex outside marriage was forbidden. Older children were often punished themselves for being complicit in sexual interaction with an adult. Until the late 18th century, there was little understanding of childhood as a concept, and children were seen as "little adults". Christianity also deemed that children were born into the original sin, and, as such, were perceived as inherently immoral. Children had very few rights and were considered the chattel of the father. From the late 18th century, and especially in the 19th century, attitudes started to change. By the mid-19th century, there was increased concern over child sexual abuse.

A general shift in social and legal attitudes toward issues of sex occurred during the modern era. Attitudes on the appropriate age of permission for females to engage in sexual activity drifted toward adulthood. While ages from 10 to 13 were typically regarded as acceptable ages for sexual consent in Western countries during the mid-19th century, by the end of the 19th century changing attitudes toward sexuality and childhood resulted in the raising of the age of consent. Several articles, written by investigative journalist William Thomas Stead in the late 19th century on the issue of child prostitution in London, led to public outrage and ultimately to the raising of the age of consent to 16. The English common law had traditionally set the age of consent within the range of 10 to 12, but in 1875 the age was raised to 13. Early feminists of the Social Purity movement, such as Josephine Butler and others, began to turn toward the problem of child prostitution by the end of the 1870s. Sensational media revelations about the scourge of child prostitution in London in the 1880s then caused outrage among the respectable middle-classes, leading to pressure for the age of consent to be raised again.

The investigative journalist William Thomas Stead of the "Pall Mall Gazette" was pivotal in exposing the problem of child prostitution in the London underworld through a publicity stunt. In 1885 he "purchased" one victim, Eliza Armstrong, the 13-year-old daughter of a chimney sweep, for five pounds and took her to a brothel where she was drugged. He then published a series of four exposés entitled "The Maiden Tribute of Modern Babylon", which shocked its readers with tales of child prostitution and the abduction, procurement, and sale of young English virgins to Continental "pleasure palaces". The "Maiden Tribute" was an instant sensation with the reading public, and Victorian society was thrown into an uproar about prostitution. Fearing riots on a national scale, the Home Secretary, Sir William Harcourt, pleaded in vain with Stead to cease publication of the articles. A wide variety of reform groups held protest meetings and marched together to Hyde Park demanding that the age of consent be raised. The government was forced to propose the Criminal Law Amendment Act 1885, which raised the age of consent to 16 and clamped down on prostitution.

In 1880s, in the United States, the most States set the minimum age at 10–12, (in Delaware it was 7 in 1895). Inspired by the "Maiden Tribute" articles, female reformers in the US initiated their own campaign which petitioned legislators to raise the legal minimum age to at least 16, with the ultimate goal to raise the age to 18. The campaign was successful, with almost all states raising the minimum age to 16–18 years by 1920. In France,

Portugal, Denmark and the Swiss cantons and other countries, the minimum age was raised to between 13 and 16 years in the following decades. Though the original arguments for raising the age of consent were based on morality, since then the raison d'être of the laws has changed to child welfare and a so-called right to childhood or innocence. In France, under the Napoleonic Code the age of consent was set in 1832 at 11, and was raised to 13 in 1863. It was increased to 15 in 1945. In Spain, it was set in 1822 at "puberty age", and changed to 12 in 1870, which was kept until 1999, when it became 13; and in 2015 it was raised to 16.

In the 21st century, concerns about child sex, tourism and commercial sexual exploitation of children gained international prominence, and have resulted in legislative changes in several jurisdictions, as well as in the adoption of several international instruments.

The Council of Europe Convention on the Protection of Children against Sexual Exploitation and Sexual Abuse (Lanzarote, 25 October 2007), and the European Union's Directive 2011/92/EU of the European Parliament and of the Council of 13 December 2011 on combating the sexual abuse and sexual exploitation of children and child pornography were adopted. The Optional Protocol on the Sale of Children, Child Prostitution and Child Pornography came into force in 2002. The Protocol to Prevent, Suppress and Punish Trafficking in Persons, especially Women and Children, which came into force in 2003, prohibits commercial sexual exploitation of children. The Council of Europe Convention on Action against Trafficking in Human Beings (which came into force in 2008) also deals with commercial sexual exploitation of children.

Several Western countries have raised their ages of consent recently. These include Canada (in 2008 - from 14 to 16); and in Europe, Iceland (in 2007 - from 14 to 15), Lithuania (in 2010 - from 14 to 16), Croatia (in 2013 - from 14 to 15), and Spain (in 2015 - from 13 to 16).

The International Criminal Court Statute does not provide a specific age of consent in its rape/sexual violence statute, but makes reference to sexual acts committed against persons "incapable of giving genuine consent"; and the explicative footnote states, "It is understood that a person may be incapable of giving genuine consent if affected by natural, induced or age-related incapacity." Sexual relations with a person under the age of consent is a crime in most countries. Jurisdictions use a variety of terms for the offense, including child sexual abuse, statutory rape, illegal carnal knowledge, corruption of a minor, besides others.

The enforcement practices of age-of-consent laws vary depending on the social sensibilities of the each particular culture. Often, enforcement is not exercised to the letter of the law, with legal action being taken only when a sufficiently socially-unacceptable age gap exists between the two individuals, or if the perpetrator is in a position of power over the minor, for example as a teacher, minister, or doctor. The sex of each participant can also influence perceptions of an individual's guilt and therefore enforcement.

Some jurisdictions, such as the Bahamas, Bermuda, Cayman Islands, Chile, Paraguay and Vanuatu have a higher age of consent for same-sex sexual activity. In both the United Kingdom and Western Australia, for example, the age of consent was originally 21 for same-sex sexual activity between males (with no laws regarding lesbian sexual activities), while it was 16 for heterosexual sexual activity; this is no longer the case. However, such discrepancies are increasingly being challenged. In Canada, the age of consent for anal sex is officially higher at 18 years, compared with 16 years for vaginal and oral sex. In the five Canadian provinces of British Columbia, Nova Scotia, Alberta, Ontario and Quebec, this discrepancy has been declared unconstitutional by courts.

In some jurisdictions, such as Indonesia, there are different ages of consent for heterosexual sexual activity that are based on the gender of each person. In countries where there are gender-age differentials, the age of consent may be higher for girls. For example in Papua New Guinea, where the age of consent for heterosexual sex is 16 for girls and 14 for boys, or they may be higher for males, such as in Indonesia, where males must be 19 years old and females must be 16 years old. There are also numerous jurisdictions, such as Kuwait and the Palestinian Territories, in which marriage laws govern the gender-age differential. In these jurisdictions, it is illegal to have sexual intercourse outside of marriage so the de facto age of consent is the marriageable age. In Kuwait, this means that boys must be at least 17 and girls at least 15 years old.

In several jurisdictions, it is illegal to engage in sexual activity with a person under a certain age under certain circumstances regarding the relationship in question, such as if it involves taking advantage of or corrupting the morals of the young person. For example, while the age of consent is 14 in Germany and 16 in Canada, it is illegal in both countries to engage in sexual activity with a person under 18 if the activity exploits the younger person. Another example is in Mexico, where there is a crime called "estupro" defined as sexual activity with a person over the age of consent but under a certain age limit (generally 18) in which consent of the younger person was obtained through seduction and/or deceit. In Pennsylvania, the age of consent is officially 16 but if the older partner is 18 or older, s/he may still be prosecuted for corruption of minors if s/he corrupts or tends to corrupt the morals of the younger person.

Traditionally, many age of consent laws dealt primarily with men engaging in sexual acts with underage girls and boys, the latter acts often falling under sodomy and buggery laws. This means that in some legal systems, women having sexual contact with underage youth were rarely acknowledged. For example, until 2000, in the UK, before the "Sexual Offences Amendment Act 2000", there was no statutory age of consent for lesbian sex. In New Zealand, before 2005, there were no age of consent laws dealing with women having sex with underage boys. Previously, in Fiji, male offenders of child sexual abuse could receive up to life imprisonment, whilst female offenders would receive up to seven years. Situations like these have been attributed to societal views on traditional gender roles, and to constructs of male sexuality and female sexuality; according to E Martellozzo, "Viewing females as perpetrators of sexual abuse goes against every stereotype that society has of women: women as mothers and caregivers and not as people who abuse and harm". Alissa Nutting argued that women are not acknowledged as perpetrators of sex crimes because society does not accept that women have an autonomous sexuality of their own.

4

Ages of Consent
Worldwide Today

To better understand what happened to Milo Yiannopoulos and where our civilization is actually heading, let's check what the current ages of consent are around the globe. The ages of consent in Africa ranges from age 12 to age 18. Angola - 12. Burkina Faso, Comoros, Niger, Sahrawi Arab Democratic Republic - 13. Botswana (Males), Cape Verde, Chad, Democratic Republic of the Congo (Females), Lesotho, Madagascar Madeira

(Portugal), São Tomé and Príncipe - 14. French Southern and Antarctic Lands (France), Îles Éparses (France), Guinea, Mayotte (France), Réunion (France) - 15. Algeria, Botswana (Females), Cameroon, Ceuta (Spain), Canary Islands, Ghana, Guinea-Bissau, Mauritania, Melilla (Spain), Malawi, Mauritius, Mozambique, Namibia (Girls), Plazas de soberanía (Spain), Senegal, South Africa, Saint Helena, Ascension and Tristan da Cunha (United Kingdom), Swaziland, Togo, Zambia, Zimbabwe - 16. Benin, Burundi, Central African Republic, Côte d'Ivoire, Democratic Republic of the Congo (Males), Djibouti, Egypt, Equatorial Guinea, Eritrea, Ethiopia, Gabon, Gambia, Kenya, Liberia, Mali, Morocco, Nigeria, Republic of the Congo, Rwanda, Seychelles, Sierra Leone, South Sudan, Somalia, Tanzania, Tunisia, Uganda - 18. Libya, Sudan - must be married.

The ages of consent in Asia range from 9 to 18. Afghanistan - 10 for men and 9 for women. Bahrain - 21 for both sexes. Bangladesh - 14. Bhutan - 18. Brunei - 16. Cambodia - 15. Hong- Kong - 16, Macau - 14. Cyprus - 17. East Timor - 14. India - 18. Indonesia - 17. Iran - 18 for men and 15 for women. Iraq - 18. Israel - 16. Japan - 13. Jordan - 16. Kuwait - 15. Kyrgystan - 16. Laos - 15. Lebanon - 18. Malaysia - 16. Maldives - 18. Mongolia - 16. Myanmar - 14. Nepal - 16. North Korea - 15. Oman - 15. Pakistan - marriage for men is 18, for women it is 16. Palestinian Territories: Gaza Strip - sex without marriage is illegal, West Bank - 16. Philippines - 12. Qatar - marriage age for men is 18, for women it is 16. Saudi Arabia - sex without marriage is illegal, marriage age 18. Singapore - 16. South Korea - age of consent is 13. Shri Lanka - 16. Syria - 15. Taiwan - 16. Tajikistan - 16. Thailand - 15. Turkmenistan - 16. United Arab Emirates - sex without marriage is illegal. Uzbekistan - 16. Vietnam - 16. Yemen - 15.

The ages of consent in Europe range from 14 to 18 years old. In Albania, Andorra, Austria, Bulgaria, Bosnia and Herzegovina, Estonia, Germany, Hungary, Italy, Liechtenstein, Macedonia, Montenegro, Portugal, San Marino, Serbia - 14. In Croatia, Czech Republic, Denmark, France, Greece, Iceland, Monaco, Poland, Romania, Slovakia, Slovenia, Sweden - 15 years old. In Armenia, Azerbaijan, Belarus, Belgium, Finland, Georgia,

Kazakhstan, Kosovo, Latvia, Lithuania, Luxembourg, Moldova, Netherlands, Northern Cyprus, Norway, Russia, Spain, Switzerland, Ukraine, United Kingdom it is 16. In Cyprus, Ireland - 17 and in Malta, Turkey, Vatican City - 18.

The ages of consent in North America for sexual activity vary by jurisdiction. In Canada it is 16, and all the US states set their limits between 16 and 18 years old. in Antigua and Barbuda, the age of consent is 16. in Anguilla (United Kingdom) - 16. In Aruba - 15. In the Bahamas - 16 for opposite sex and 18 for same sex, but "public homosexuality" is an offence that carries 20-yesr jail term without parole. In Barbados - 16. In Belize - 16. in Bermuda and British Virgin Islands (United Kingdom) - 16. In Canada - 16. Cayman Islands (United Kingdom) - 16. Caribbean Netherlands - 16. Costa Rica - 18. Cuba - 16. Curaçao (Netherlands) - 15. Dominica - 16. Dominican Republic - 18. El Salvador - 18. Greenland (Denmark) has Denmark laws. Grenada - 16. Guadeloupe (France) - has France's laws. Guatemala - 18 yeas years old. Haiti - 18. Honduras - 14. Jamaica - 16. Martinique (France) has France's laws. Mexico - 12-18 with some restrictions and there is a chance of being prosecuted under certain circumstances.

The ages of consent in Oceania ranging from 15 to 18 years old with some exemptions. Australia is a federation of States and Territories, with each State and Territory having the primary jurisdiction over age of consent issues within its territory. The Australian Capital Territory, Coral Sea Islands, New South Wales and Norfolk Island, Northern Territory, Queensland, Victoria, Western Australia age of consent is 16. In South Australia, Tasmania - 17. In Clipperton Island (France) the general age of consent is 15. Easter Island (Chile) has the South America's laws. In Federated States of Micronesia, the states' statutory rape laws apply to children age 13 and below in Chuuk, Yap, and Kosrae, and age of 15 and below in Pohnpei. Fiji's age of consent is 16. French Polynesia (France) and Kiribati - 15. Juan Fernández Islands (Chile) has South America's laws. The Marcus Island (Japan) and Okinotori Islands (Japan) are under the government of Japan. Marshall Islands, Nauru, New Zealand, Cook Islands, Tokelau - 16. New Caledonia (France) has French laws. Palau - 17. Papua (Indonesia) has

Indonesia's laws. Papua New Guinea - 16 for women and 14 for men. Pitcairn Island (United Kingdom) and Samoa - 16. Tonga, Tuvalu - 15. Northern Mariana Islands - 18. Pacific Remote Islands Marine National Monument and Midway Atoll are under the jurisdiction of the US Federal laws. Vanuatu's age of consent is 15. Wallis and Futuna (France) has the French laws.

Many countries have the close-in-age exemptions that should be explained separately. Ages of consent laws regarding sexual activity in the United States set at the state level. There are several federal statutes related to protecting minors from sexual predators, but laws regarding specific age requirements for sexual consent are left to individual states, territories, and the District of Columbia. In Alabama, Alaska, Arkansas, Connecticut, Georgia, Hawaii, Indiana, Iowa, Kansas, Kentucky, Maine, Maryland, Massachusetts, Michigan, Minnesota, Mississippi, Montana, Nebraska, Nevada, New Hampshire, New Jersey, North Carolina, Ohio, Oklahoma, Pennsylvania, Rhode Island, South Carolina, South Dakota, Vermont, Washington, and West Virginia the age of consent is 16. In California (some exceptions if sex with a spouse), Arizona, Delaware, Florida, Idaho, North Dakota, Oregon, Tennessee, Utah, Virginia, Wisconsin - 18. Colorado, Illinois, Louisiana, Missouri, New Mexico, New York, Texas, Wyoming - 17. American Samoa, Guam, Puerto Rico - 16. Northern Mariana Islands, United States Virgin Islands - 18 years old. The United States Minor Outlying Islands are under jurisdiction of the US Federal Government. And again, almost all the US's states have the close-in-age exemptions just like almost all countries worldwide.

The largest gap between ages of consent is in Asia, it is 9 in Afghanistan (for women) and 21 in Bahrain.

5

Islam, Sharia Law
& Sexual Activities

In such Islamic countries as Libya, Sudan, Palestinian Territories Gaza Strip, United Arab Emirates, and Saudi Arabia, the sexual activities without marriage are not permitted. And it is strange that the Sharia law, which is Islam, is now widely promoted in the US by the sexually-obsessed left, who probably do not understand that Islam laws would bring their restrictions into every country where Sharia and Islam laws would be established. And they would be permitting sexual activities only after marriage or only with a…

41

woman-slave. Women slavery in 21st century, does the left want THIS? There are many more other interesting details related to the subject of sexuality, which the Americans who promote Islam in the US have no knowledge about.

The Islamic sexual jurisprudence concerns the Islamic laws of sexuality as largely predicated on the Qur'an, the sayings of Muhammad and the rulings of religious leaders, which confine sexual activity to heterosexual marital sexual relations between one Muslim male and no more than one wife at a time from up to four concurrent lawful wives (Muslim or otherwise); or heterosexual marital sexual relations between one Muslim female and her one sole lawful Muslim husband; or heterosexual concubinage sexual relations between one Muslim male slave-owner and no more than one female slave at a time from any number of concurrently wholly owned female slaves, Muslim or otherwise. Sexual activity itself is not to be considered a taboo subject in Islam, although there are strong prohibitions against both male and female Muslims engaging in sex outside of marriage and, for male Muslims, sex with a female non-spouse, that is not a wholly owned female slave, i.e. shared-ownership. Permissible sexual relationships are described in Quran and Hadith as great wells of love and closeness. Even within marriage and concubinage, there are limitations: a man should not have intercourse during his wife's or female slave's menstruation and afterbirth periods. He is also considered to be sinning when penetrating anally. Actions and behaviors such as abortion, other than for medical risk to the pregnant woman, and homosexuality are also strictly forbidden; contraceptive use is permitted for birth control.

What would have happen to Hollywood if the US suddenly adopted the Sharia law? It would be the end to the "shining like diamonds" rotten tomatoes' community of California. Literally and figuratively. Logically, all gays, lesbians, transgenders, feminists, and those constantly involved in adultery, swinging, sex orgies, etc. etc. etc. should praise Yiannopoulos for speaking out against Islam. Sure, he often doesn't flatter the ears of gays, feminists and transgenders too, but that just the words that should make them think, not to get mad. They should learn to analyze things.

If you are a feminist, imagine what would happen if Islam laws were adopted in the US. There would be the patriarchy here, women would have no freedoms they currently have. What would happen to outspoken you, wearing a ring in your nose? You would be under a heavy pressure of Islamic laws that would make you obey males you desperately hate, and there would be also no piercing and many other things you like. Even if you are not a feminist, you still would have no way to survive the Islamic laws without "casualties", especially if you would marry a Muslim guy. My mother - Vera (in translation from Russian "Faith") - was not happy with her marriage to a Muslim man. She was a woman with the Christian values, a very nice, kind person. Europe-born, with the red hair and green eyes, she was well educated, stubborn, loved to experiment. No wonder she fell in love with a Muslim and married him. And it was okay, but only until she appeared with her husband in a Muslim's community. Under pressure of his family and friends he started treating her according to Sharia laws and it was unacceptable. In a Muslim world, a female is not an equal "creature". Female is not a human in Muslim's world. There was no way for my mother to get a divorce, and she took a small bag with her tooth brush and a spare dress, said that she wanted to go visit her friends. She left and never came back. Several years later, she met my father, Ivan, who was a military officer, atheist and liked Stalin. She married him. Even they were very different, they lived together for the rest of their lives. And it was more harmonic marriage comparing to what happened to her when she married a Muslim. According to my mom's words, her ex-Muslim husband was a nice guy, but he did not treat her right because he had to follow the Islamic religious rules, rituals, and canons to fit in the Islamic community lifestyle. He knew that this was unacceptable to her, but he could not change anything because he was under a heavy pressure from his relatives, males friends, community customs, and laws in general. She said to me that the European woman cannot live according those laws. However, when with my father Ivan, she did not worry about the male-female inequality and wearing or not wearing hijab. The CPA by education, she eventually got settled in a high-paying but boring job, such as a director of a food store, while my father was (after he retired from the military) the director of a large auto repair company. Both had the high-paying jobs in the ex-USSR, but they could not buy the right to free speech and the liberties, which were the unreachable luxury in the Soviet Union.

There is no reason for Islamophobia, however, we should realize that not everything is simple in this world. We need to remember our own roots and be proud of them, be proud for who we are without any switching to something "better" to eventually end up in a living hell. There is a wise old saying: "There're different strokes for different folks." If you disagree, then stop sleeping or smocking and start thinking about everything, including who needed legalization of dope last few years.

By arguing against adopting Islam in America Milo is trying to protect first of all himself as a gay (who doesn't mind to get eventually straight according to his word) and then also all those, who would not fit in with the Sharia law for many different reasons, you. There are too many of you, who would not fit in, including the Catholics, Jews, atheists, feminists, LGTB, arguing for abortion democrats, the regular American women, who love to be equal with men, just all freedom-loving individuals. Then who does need the Islamic laws in America and why? Only those who are the Muslims, who are (still) the minority. And what would the Muslim world offer to America in exchange? The Christian's and Jewish's United Arab Emirates and the LGTB's and feminist's Saudi Arabia? That's not going to happen. Muslims want rule the whole world but it's not going to happen too.

There are more facts there related to Islam. The founder of religion of Islam was Muhammad, who was accepted by Muslims throughout the world as the last of the prophets of God. Muhammad was born in 570, in Mecca, Arabia (now Saudi Arabia) and died June 8, 632, in Medina. According to Sunni scriptural Hadith sources, a girl Aisha was six or seven years old when she was married to Muhammad, with the marriage not being consummated until she had reached puberty at the age of nine or ten years old. It seems that many Democrats just love some historical Islamic facts and want make them the US's laws.

6

Why Do We Need Freedom of Speech

These days, a British man Yannopoulos is much better at exercising his right to free speech in the US than many Americans, who almost forgot that they have a fundamental right to free speech, the 1st Amendment. The political correctness filters made intellectually blind almost everyone. When we do not speak our mind and do not hear others speaking their mind, we lose our ability to think and analyze reality, we start thinking just like we talk, avoiding the sharp angles, avoiding the truth. It is a victimization by the "political correctness". Imagine a doctor, who would lose his mind, just like the left, and would start "respect" germs and what they do to our bodies. He would call it "political correctness" because his little brothers germs are also the living creatures. However, even he could experiment with his own body's germs (some doctors of the past heroically sacrificed themselves to invent new medications), he has no right to let deadly creatures grow in the bodies of his patients. If a doctor would "respect" germs, seeing them as the victims (of the healing process), the patients would eventually die from the illness. The truth is health, political correctness - germs, because it is created by the lies and because it hurts reality and healthy body of our society. We need healthy society. And only the truth can expose the germs of society. Our society is in need of the curing.

We, our lives, and the reality are in a continuous transformation. Tomorrow would be another day, with other positive and negative experiences. Some feminist girl might get lucky and meet a fascinating straight guy that would rock her world, changing her views in a minute. A gay guy might meet some amazing straight girl, who would be able to unintentionally convert him into a straight male with an unpredictable ease. An individual with the socialist-communist views might eventually understand that s/he was brainwashed. Nobody knows. Nothing is forever. We never know what future would bring, but we constantly label each other. For sure, we all must have our personal opinions or even views on everything, which can be different than those that our neighbors have. We all grew up in absolutely different conditions, we have absolutely different life experiences and knowledge. We cannot think similar and should not hate each other for thinking differently. We should be able to express freely ourselves, our views and opinions about our positive and negative experiences in life. Yes, opinions would be positive and negative, just like the experiences. We also want to be heard and understood without expecting that a Molotov cocktail would blow us up. The Molotov cocktail has been used mostly in 3rd world countries by the street criminals, gangsters, urban guerrillas, terrorists, and by the rioters… at

Berkeley as an equivalent to military-issue weapon. It never has been used by intellectuals, who can express their thoughts civilize way. If you do not like something, find the truth peacefully. We are not the animals, we still can read and talk, and the US is still not the ISIS territory.

7
World We Live In
& World We Want

We all know that there is always some particular world order exists and that there are the people who rule or at least who are trying to rule. If a person does not obey the established rules (even if they are not the best) and is trying to establish his/her new rules, the old "powers" will try to "demolish" this annoying newcomer, one way or another, as someone who doesn't fit in. Sexual accusations are the most powerful accusations because they can damage reputation easily. And majority of people often believe those accusations without any actual proof. Many people still believe the striking and suggestive titles of today's mainstream media fake news' articles which protect already established "world order." February 2017, Milo Yiannopoulos found himself in between, smashed by two large groups, by the leftists, who were in a deadly agony, and by the Conservatives, who were establishing themselves as a new power.

Should we criticize Milo? His mission is to drain the swamp, accompanying it with his laughs and sometimes theatrical appearances. Was his reputation demolished by the accusations? No one believes he is a pedophile or supports pedophilia. And it is obvious that he did not expect those attacks. Yiannopoulos was victimized by those who felt that he went too far, even he was not a pedophile and he did not support the pedophilia. As the Chapter 2 said, Milo was 13 when he was engaged in sexual activities for the first time. He was sexually mature at this age, and even called himself a "predator." So finding a partner should be a normal consequence. And he got one. However, this one was a real predator, because he was older and knew what he was doing. Unfortunately things went wrong for Milo and he grew up with a feeling that in his 13 he was a grown man, even he obviously was a victim. But does he deserve the punishment he has received later?

Everything that has happened to Yiannopoulos during February of 2017 is a nonsense and majority realizes it. Another thing, Milo understands that to be a gay is abnormality, and it really is. It is widely known that males become gays because they as children were sexually abused by the gays adults. Too bad, in the contemporary US it became "fashionable" to be a gay. This happened only during the Obama presidency. However, it looks silly to many people when the young men want to be gays just because, according the highly suggestive fake news mainstream media, to be a gay is a good thing. It is actually more comedic thing, humorous thing, sarcastic thing, playing women thing. It could be just an experiment (not necessary one), but not forever. Sure it is often not easy to be a man, especially when you get older, like Caitlyn Jenner. But you should have the guts, guys. And who could know that it is such a privilege to be a woman. It is amazing to see how many men want to be women. They dress like women, walk like women, they even fight against real females for a space under sun. However, men should be proud of their nature, strength and ability to do things women cannot, not opposite.

Now I feel that someone is ready to throw a Molotov cocktail into the author of this chapter. You cannot do this, sorry. Just drop it, stop it. We are not the monkeys. Facts first, feelings later.

8

Who is Milo?

Milo Yannopoulos (Milo Hanrahan) is a public speaker, media personality, and a former senior editor for Breitbart News. He has written under the pen name Milo Andreas Wagner. Yiannopoulos co-founded The Kernel in 2011, an online tabloid magazine about technology, which he sold to Daily Dot Media in 2014. As a cultural libertarian and free speech fundamentalist, he is a vocal critic of movements and ideologies he deems authoritarian or belonging to the "regressive" left.

Yiannopoulos considers himself a reporter of and "occasional fellow traveler" with the alt-right movement. In July 2016, he was banned from Twitter for what the company cited as "inciting or engaging in the targeted abuse or harassment of others." However, many others would say that Milo simply was exercising his right to free speech, which is not unlawful in the US. In February 2017, he resigned from Breitbart after a controversy arising from a video at "Drunken Peasants," where he said that sexual relationships between "younger boys" and "older men" could be a positive experience for the boys (Milo mentioned his own experience with a priest Michael). He resigned from Breitbart after both his speech at CPAC and his book "Dangerous" were canceled because of the same video. The "Dangerous" was already #1 bestselling book at Amazon (pre-order) at the moment of its cancellation.

A few days later, March 4, the chairman of ACU Matt Schlapp explained in his interview why he disinvited Milo Yiannopoulos from CPAC. He said that he was negatively influenced by a widely circulating "Drunken Peasants" video, felt uncomfortable to be around a criminal, he did not know Milo that well. However, he recently had a conversation with Yiannopoulos and doesn't believe that he supports pedophilia. Schlapp said that he would give him a chance to explain himself.

Almost at the same time, Joy Villa, the #1 Artist with best-selling album on iTunes, who shocked everyone at the Grammy Awards with her dress "Make America Great Again", said that what has happened to Milo is not fair and that they butcher him for nothing. She said that she loves Milo and supports him, and that what happened to him "did not diminish his light at all, ...someone else would pick up his book. He is an icon." Joy Villa, who supports Donald Trump, recommended Milo not to worry about anything because they are going to attack him for no matter what. Villa's companion Andre Soriano, who is a Filipino-born American fashion designer and a creator of her "Make America Great Again" dress, added, "We love Milo, M-I-L-O!"

Milo is the one of the Youtube's not average users, his videos have a tremendous number of views.

What is the attraction and what is he talking about? The following couple of pages will describe what Milo said during some of his speeches. Basically this chapter is for those who do not have the access to Internet or for that occasion when Internet would be shut down. Thinking logically, if someone wants to shut down people like Milo Yiannopoulos, Ann Coulter, Lauren Southern, they probably would want to shut down Internet too. Wow, what a talk! How did America even get up there? But it seems that all traditional views are not acceptable by the left any more.

Milo talks about everything related to his life and the world he lives in, and often he does is in a humorous manner to make a better connection with his audience or to provoke or encourage the critical thinking. For example he can dress up as a drag queen for the Q&A event, and when someone in the audience would ask him a question, "Are your tits even?", Milo would try to fix his fake breasts and then would say, "…This is more body positivity, …they suppose to be even, but if not even, fix [them] for me." But this is not the traditional questions and answers you would hear. Regularly

Milo is very substantial during his events. He is an intellectual human being, who has not only a great sense of humor but also has actually something to say. One of the most of his important saying is that facts first, feelings secondary. And he is not trying to offend anyone, as the left suggests. It is a nonsense to be offended by the truth, by joke, or by something that doesn't not exists, like the wrong interpretation of words or their meaning. It is as if to be offended by your own lack of intellect or your own lack of sense of humor. People regularly afraid of things and people that they don't comprehend. Knowledge is power, and Milo stimulates you to move forward toward that knowledge. If you disagree with him (that's okay), make your own research, but make sure you have the all facts that can prove your point.

At the University of Central Florida, during his Q&A event, Milo answered a question giving his opinion on Pope Francis, who encouraged refugees flow in Europe, which destroys Europe. Milo said that the best Pope in history was Benedict XVI for some time and that the social justice was invented by Catholic Church, but it was twisted and inflated by progressive left. He said that even many might think that Catholic Church is a "scary conservative institution," it is in fact a very left wing. Milo invites you to follow him in the labyrinths of his thought and this following sometimes makes an explosion in a weak mind, but mostly when that "mind" is looking for any opportunity to explode (for no reason).

At the same event, asked by another person about integration of Islam into a Western world society, Milo said that Islam doesn't have enlightenment yet, which is true. However, he added that he hopes it is possible that Islam would be integrated, but he doesn't see it would be coming any time soon. Seems Milo has nothing against this integration. For those not sure what "enlightenment" is: Enlightenment is a European intellectual movement of the late 17th and 18th centuries emphasizing reason and individualism rather than tradition. It was heavily influenced by 17th-century philosophers such as Descartes, Locke, and Newton, and its prominent exponents include Kant, Goethe, Voltaire, Rousseau, and Adam Smith.

Yiannopoulos also said that the Western world has demonstrated through the freedoms, democracy, property rights, and capitalism (like America) that its values are better than "those regimes" values and this is why more countries want to become like America, so they could also flourish. But it has to come from them. When answering the Hispanic Christian conservative Jorge's question about Muslims in Palestine, Milo said that criticizing Islam is not "racists, that there is no such thing as Islamophobia, it was an invention of the left.

During another university's speech, which took place during his "Dangerous Faggot" tour, 30 days before the Presidential election, he said that friends and foes call him simply Milo and that the liberals afraid to say hard names because if they say them wrong - it is racist, if they say them right - it is a cultural appropriation. He informed the audience of how the Clinton's campaign operated, of its lies, corruption, media lies, why Hillary Clinton would change the US to worse and what would happen if she would be in charge of the Supreme Court. Milo mentioned the age range in the Supreme Court: Ruth Bader-Ginsberg - 83, Anthony Kennedy - 80,

Steven Breyer - 78, Clarence Thomas - 68, Samuel Alilo - 66, Sonia Sotomayor - 62. The average retirement age in Supreme Court is 79. The left wanted for Supreme Court more sleepiness, while Supreme Court is the most powerful people in America. He was worried about authoritarianism that was coming to America because the left thinks that "social progress" is extremely important, and to achieve it they must control what people say and what people think. The left thinks that it is normal to have one policy for their favorite groups and entirely different for others. Reason and consistency do not mean anything to the left. And it is true, who would argue? He said that a term "hate speech" was invented by the left to use it when they have no arguments, and the "hate speech" could be everything they do not like, everything that remotely could be described as libertarian, republican, and especially humor. The left sees the hate speech, racism, and sexism everywhere, and if Clinton would win, the 1st Amendment would be in a serious risk. The Milo's speeches resonate with many because many people who were victimized by the political correctness already subconsciously noticed what there is something wrong is happening in this country, even they often did not formulate those happenings in phrases as Milo did.

The Yiannopoulos' Dangerous Faggot Tour speeches took place at University of Mexico, University of Colorado Boulder, University of Washington, Minnesota State University, UW-Mulwaukee, Michigan State University, Miami University, West Virginian University, Ohio State University, Dartmouth College, UC Irvine, George Mason University, University of Delaware, George Washington University, Clemson University, Western Carolina University, University of Alabama, Auburn University, UCF, LSU, University of Houston, UC San Diego, University of California, UCLA, UCSB, De-Paul University, University of Oregon, American University, University of Pittsburg, Bucknell University, University of Michigan, Rutgers, and other venues. All these speeches are available now on Youtube.

The speech at Berkeley University has been canceled because of the violent protest that occurred on campus. The organizer of this protest was Yvette Felarca, a middle school social studies teacher, who has a history of instigating violence. She said during her interview with Tucker Carlson on Fox News that she organized this protest because Milo is a fascist. In a video posted on Youtube she said that people like Milo want threaten minorities and illegal immigrants, intimidate them, rape them, kill them. Does she realize that Milo is also a minority, he is a gay, immigrant, half Jewish. She said, "It is real. This is life and death. This is not an abstract question of who's theory are you interested in researching. This is about our lives right now." As a result, 150 masked protesters against Milo's speech at Berkeley University caused $100,000 in damage. They were acting as fascists, threatening peace of campus and of surrounding communities. There were no students among those violent protesters who threw Molotov cocktails, commercial-grade fireworks and rocks at police. They smashed windows of a student union center on the Berkeley campus, where the Yiannopoulos' event was to be held. Milo was safely evacuated, but a few people were attacked and injured. And now the logical questions have risen, such as "who are the fascists and who are not?" and "what can students learn from a teacher as Yvette Felarca and where they would end up later?" There are no excuses for what happened at Berkeley. Fascism and Yvette Felarca reject assertions that violence is automatically negative in nature and it unites them. Is there a solution to any type of conflict? The logic and respect.

To understand Yiannopoulos better but without labeling, let's check what the libertarians views are, even he probably is not a 100% libertarian as many think. According to the daily modified by leftists source, libertarianism is a collection of political philosophies that uphold liberty as a core principle. Libertarians seek to maximize autonomy and freedom of choice, emphasizing political freedom, voluntary association, and the importance of individual judgment. Libertarians often share a skepticism of authority and state power. However, they diverge on the scope of their opposition to existing political and economic systems. Various schools of libertarian thought offer a range of views regarding the legitimate functions of state and private power, often calling to restrict or to dissolve coercive social institutions.

Some libertarians advocate laissez-faire capitalism and strong private property rights, such as in land, infrastructure, and natural resources. Others, libertarian socialists, seek to abolish capitalism and private ownership of the means of production in favor of their common or cooperative ownership and management, viewing private property as a barrier to freedom and liberty. An additional line of division is between minarchists and anarchists. While minarchists think that a minimal centralized government is necessary, anarchists and anarcho-capitalists propose to completely eliminate the state.

It seems that Milo has adopted many characteristics that belong to the first category of libertarians, who support capitalism, as he loves America, private property idea, freedoms, including the right to free speech. But it would be wrong to label anyone, including Yiannopoulos, as we are more complex persons than it seems, and the majority of us searching or in self-development process.

According to same encyclopedia, a word libertarian continues to be widely used to refer to socialists internationally. However, its meaning in the US hasdeviated from its political origins. Right-libertarianism developed in the United States in the mid-20th century and is the most popular conception of libertarianism in America. Right-libertarians value the social institutions that enforce conditions of capitalism, while rejecting institutions that function in opposition to these institutions. Anarcho-capitalists seek complete elimination of the state in favor of privately funded security services, while minarchists defend "night-watchman states", which maintain only those functions of government necessary to maintain conditions of capitalism.

Now I hear some voice that criticizes the "white males." But the US was created by the white males. The Founding Fathers of the United States were the white men of the Thirteen British Colonies in North America who led the American Revolution against authority of the British Crown and established the United States of America. The term Founding Fathers is used more narrowly, referring specifically to those who either signed the Declaration of Independence in 1776 or who were delegates to the 1787 Constitutional Convention and took part in drafting the proposed Constitution of the United States. A further subset includes those who signed the Continental Association or the Articles of Confederation. During much of the 19th century, they were referred to as either the "Founders" or the "Fathers". Historian Richard B. Morris in 1973 identified the following seven figures as the key Founding Fathers: John Adams, Benjamin Franklin, Alexander Hamilton, John Jay, Thomas Jefferson, James Madison, and George Washington. Adams, Jefferson, and Franklin worked on the committee to draft the Declaration of Independence. Hamilton, Madison, and Jay were authors of the The Federalist Papers, advocating ratification of the Constitution. Washington commanded the revolutionary army. All served in important positions in the early government of the United States.

Normally, the people who live in America should be thankful to the Founding Fathers who created such a great country, obviously the best country in the world. They were, no doubts, geniuses (and Rh negative). And there is a final question: Why we should let anyone with lesser amount of the gray matter and with the lack of history's knowledge make even minor changes or corrections to the fabulous US's Constitution, created by geniuses? Just love and respect what you have, no further "inventions," no cave's thinking. And even if someone does not like white men any more, they are great if not the best because they created the US, a country of freedoms and liberties.

CONCLUSION

To be ready for globalization, the all people need enlightenment. And here are the *NeoPopRealist 10 Canons for happier life,* created by artist Nadia Russ in 2004, just as this book was written by her in 2017, that could actually help. Every culture, religion and ideology must be ready for integration. However, now, because so many people are possessed by negativity, which came from the personal regress happened as a result of choosing the wrong path, we are not ready for globalization. All graduates from the beyonce's academy have tendency to be negative. Never satisfied with anything, they throw their darkness on everybody else, playing the blame game while trying to hurt others in a fight for superiority. Led by negativity and negative people, globalization today would be a civilization's collapssiation. The "collapssiation" is a new word (but not 100% new), invented specially for this book. Isn't this so democratic? Actually an idea of globalization is a great idea but only if there would be no surveillance and no Satanic government. Too bad the people are not ready for it (yet) and Soros wants to see it happened today, because he is already 87. So much time wasted.

Americans need to get together to overcome all obstacles, created by a previous big spender and vacations lover president Obama, and make America great again. The whole world needs it, sure except those who can focus only on "pizza" with "hot dogs" (see WikiLeaks for decoding) or Quran.

NeoPopRealism 10 Canons for Happier Life: 1. Be beautiful. 2. Be creative. 3. Be peace-loving, positive-minded. 4. Do not accept communist philosophy. 5. Be free-minded, do the best you can to move the world to peace and harmony. 6. Be family oriented, self-disciplined. 7. Be free-spirited. Follow your dreams if they are not destructive but constructive. 8. Believe in god. God is one, it is harmony and striving for perfection. 9. Be supportive to those who need you, be generous. 10. Create your life as a great adventurous story.

March 2017
(slightly edited June 2017)

~Notes ~